A MAN in Deo Toolkit

Con̶nec̶tin̶g men with Jesus

Andy Gower

otlt

Connecting men with Jesus

 Published by: On the line training, Sheffield, UK.
Email: books@otlt.org

First published June 2014

ISBN: 978-0-9929130-0-7

Printed by DS Print & Design, Sheffield, UK.

"I pray that you may be active in sharing your faith,

so that you will have a full understanding

of every good thing that we have in Christ."

Paul's letter to Philemon, verse 6.

Acknowledgements:

Over several years of seeking to follow Jesus there have been so many helpful influencers that it is difficult to know who to thank and how to itemise their contributions.

The family of Speen Baptist Church (from 1996 to 2011) was the crucible in which some of the concepts in this toolkit were formed as a necessary response to our missional situation.

The Baptist family in the UK have supported and shaped me in ministry, and I am very grateful for their wise input over the years.

Neil Anderson's spiritual insights have been carefully adapted for the UK by Steve Goss and the team at Freedom in Christ Ministries. These resources were a foundational tool in forming fruitful disciples at Speen.

Mike Breen, Paul Maconochie and Rich Robinson at 3DM have blessed the Church internationally with both the discipling concepts of Lifeshapes and the Huddle format that facilitates disciples walking together. Carolyn and I are most grateful to them and to Andy Stone for taking us under their wing and Huddling us.

Carl Beech at Christian Vision for Men has pioneered a refreshing approach to men's ministry. Without Carl and our Indian partners, Sekhar & Chandra, this project would not have seen the light of day.

Then there are many other friends and family members who have given unstintingly of their time and resources, and upheld us in their prayers. You know who you are - thank you!

Finally, but most importantly, it is all about Jesus. He has called us into his family and made us partners in the *missio Dei*. We pray he gets all the glory from this little book.

Contents

The Mystery of the Missing Men

How many men are there regularly attending your church?

How many men are there compared with the number of regular woman attendees?

In many churches there are far fewer men than women. This imbalance has had a significant negative impact on the effectiveness of the Church, particularly in regard to mission. For example, an article published in the USA[1] suggests that a man is the most effective member of the family in bringing the whole family to the Lord:

> If you lead a child to Christ, in 3% of the cases the family follows.
>
> If you lead a mother to Christ, in 17% of the cases the family follows.
>
> If you lead a father to Christ, in 93% of the cases the family follows.

How can we find them?

There are many reasons for the lack of men in our churches. This Toolkit deals with some of them. The Toolkit enables men to establish authentic friendships both within and beyond their local church:

> Authentic friendships through which Jesus disciples them.
>
> Authentic friendships as the network for sharing Jesus with other men.
>
> Authentic friendships through which those men who discover Jesus, are then discipled by him with others.

How you can gather them

Run the two Programmes in this Toolkit with a group of men in your church. Each Programme consists of six Sessions and each Session lasts for approximately 90 minutes.

The Programmes are designed to connect your group to Jesus and connect you to each other through structured sessions of fun, food and study.

Together you will learn to talk and listen to Jesus, experience his life changing power and recognise how to impact for good the lives of those around you.

The first Programme develops the shared identity and cohesiveness of the group - building a Band of Brothers.

The second Programme leads this Band of Brothers through the model for evangelism that Jesus trained his followers to use, and shows how the group can do this themselves.

When used together, these two Programmes provide a discipleship framework to:

Equip men to follow Jesus together.

Resource men to reach out to other men with the good news of Jesus.

Enable men to engage in changing their communities and society for the better.

Once you and the group have run the Programmes you will be well on your way to gathering men. You will have seen how a network of men draws other men towards Jesus and learnt the freedom of being his disciples.

Mutual discipleship within authentic friendships is the key - men being disciples of Jesus together.

A Normal Session

The Sessions are designed to run weekly or fortnightly. A 90 minute Session consists of two parts:

Part 1 - Social Time

The goal of this part of the Session is to build friendships. More learning will take place when time is given to having fun together.

The first 30 minutes is for games, e.g. volleyball, frisbee, or board games, followed by 15 minutes for drinks and snacks.

Session 6 of each Programme is set around a meal.

Part 2 - Study Time

The goal of this part of the Session is to engage together with Jesus.

Each Study Time is designed to last for 45 minutes and consists of Bible reading, discussion and prayer. The group will learn about Jesus and learn to share their lives.

For the Study Time the men need to be in groups of between 4 and 8 men. The groups should have the same people in them for every Session.

Leaders Notes

To help you get the best from the Sessions Leaders Notes are provided in Appendix 2. Please use these prayerfully.

This Toolkit is not a method; it is designed to enable relationship building with Jesus and each other.

Programme 1:

Growing as a Band of Brothers

Welcome to Programme 1!

Special Instructions for Programme 1

The group will learn about being disciples of Jesus together.

As the Programme progresses relationships in your group will deepen and you will realise the importance of following Jesus in relationship with others, so be prepared for the dynamics in the group to change.

About the 'Read' Sections

Please use the Bible passages in the Toolkit (and not from someones' preferred version). They are intentionally in 'common' language - just as the original Gospels were.

Social Time

The 45 minutes Social Time before the Study Time is vital to building friendship. You will learn more together if you do this well.

Session 6 takes place around a meal. It needs to be planned ahead of time.

(Don't forget to prayerfully read the Leaders Notes in Appendix 2).

Session 1: Jesus is our Lord

Part 1: Social Time

Games:

Drinks and Snack:

Part 2: Study Time

Focus 1:

Read: Luke 5:1-11

One day as Jesus was standing by the Lake of Gennesaret, the people were crowding round him and listening to the word of God. [2]He saw at the water's edge two boats, left there by the fishermen, who were washing their nets. [3]He got into one of the boats, the one belonging to Simon, and asked him to put out a little from the shore. Then he sat down and taught the people from the boat.

[4]When he had finished speaking, he said to Simon, 'Put out into deep water, and let down the nets for a catch.'

[5]Simon answered, 'Master, we've worked hard all night and haven't caught anything. But because you say so, I will let down the nets.'

[6]When they had done so, they caught such a large number of fish that their nets began to break. [7]So they signalled to their partners in the other boat to come and help them, and they came and filled both boats so full

that they began to sink.

[8]When Simon Peter saw this, he fell at Jesus' knees and said, 'Go away from me, Lord; I am a sinful man!' [9]For he and all his companions were astonished at the catch of fish they had taken, [10]and so were James and John, the sons of Zebedee, Simon's partners.Then Jesus said to Simon, 'Don't be afraid; from now on you will fish for people.' [11]So they pulled their boats up on shore, left everything and followed him.

Think:

Peter is doing his everyday job as a fisherman.

He is an experienced and skilled fisherman on the Lake of Gennesaret (also called the Sea of Galilee). He knows when and how to catch fish there.

Jesus shows his miraculous power over something that Peter was an expert in.

Peter recognises that Jesus has authority over the natural world, falls down in worship, and is honest about his own sinful condition and need of forgiveness.

Jesus calls Peter to follow him - and gives Peter's life a new direction and purpose.

Discuss:

Tell each other what the word 'Lord' means to you?

How does following Jesus give you hope and a purpose for your life?

Focus 2:

Read: Acts 4:5-13

⁵The next day the rulers, the elders and the teachers of the law met in Jerusalem. ⁶Annas the high priest was there, and so were Caiaphas, John, Alexander and others of the high priest's family. ⁷They had Peter and John brought before them and began to question them: 'By what power or what name did you do this?'

⁸Then Peter, filled with the Holy Spirit, said to them: 'Rulers and elders of the people! ⁹If we are being called to account today for an act of kindness shown to a man who was lame and are being asked how he was healed, ¹⁰then know this, you and all the people of Israel: it is by the name of Jesus Christ of Nazareth, whom you crucified but whom God raised from the dead, that this man stands before you healed. ¹¹Jesus is:

"The stone you builders rejected, which has become the cornerstone."

¹²Salvation is found in no one else, for there is no other name under heaven given to mankind by which we must be saved.'

¹³When they saw the courage of Peter and John and realised that they were unschooled, ordinary men, they were astonished and they took note that these men had been with Jesus.

Think:

Peter has been arrested for healing a lame man and preaching about Jesus. After a night in prison he is on trial before the leaders of his nation - the same people who had crucified Jesus only weeks earlier.

Peter trusts God for the outcome.

He challenges the action of the leaders and explains the unique importance of Jesus.

The leaders are angry but surprised at Peter's courage, then they recognise that he has been trained by Jesus.

Discuss:

How is Jesus different from other leaders?

How long have you been following Jesus?

How has Jesus been changing/training you?

Action:

What are you concerned, worried, or anxious about?

Share it in your group, then together ask Jesus to show his power over this thing.

A Prayer:

Jesus, you called Peter to follow you,

And I know you are calling me to follow you too.

It's difficult for me to give up being in control of my life,

because I've been running it my way for a long time.

Jesus, I know you can be trusted.

So today I choose to let you lead me,

- you can have my life, all of it.

I want to be your disciple,

I will follow you, ... Lord Jesus.

Session 2: God is our Father

Part 1: Social Time

Games:

Drinks and Snack:

Part 2: Study Time

Focus 1:

Read: Matthew 6:5-9

5'And when you pray, do not be like the hypocrites, for they love to pray standing in the synagogues and on the street corners to be seen by others. Truly I tell you, they have received their reward in full.

6But when you pray, go into your room, close the door and pray to your Father, who is unseen. Then your Father, who sees what is done in secret, will reward you.

7And when you pray, do not keep on babbling like pagans, for they think they will be heard because of their many words. 8Do not be like them, for your Father knows what you need before you ask him.

9"This, then, is how you should pray:

"Our Father in heaven, hallowed be your name,..."'

Think:

Jesus describes the relationship we have with God as that of a 'loving Father and trusting child'.

Jesus' disciples are like children who can speak openly and directly to Father God about everything and anything.

Discuss:

What was your relationship with your earthly father like?

Has this been a help or a hindrance to understanding the loving Father-trusting child relationship we have with God?

Focus 2:

Read: John's Gospel 1:12-13 and the First Letter of John 3:1-2

[12] Yet to all who did receive him, to those who believed in his name, he gave the right to become children of God —[13]children born not of natural descent, nor of human decision or a husband's will, but born of God.

John 1:12-13

See what great love the Father has lavished on us, that we should be called children of God! And that is what we are!

The reason the world does not know us is that it did not know him.

2Dear friends, now we are children of God, and what we will be has not yet been made known. But we know that when Christ appears, we shall be like him, for we shall see him as he is.

1 John 3:1-2

Think:

These Bible passages describe how those who accept Jesus as Lord become children of God.

God has brought us to spiritual rebirth - he wants a family!

The writer says Father God *lavishes* his love on us.

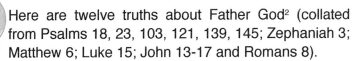

Action:

Here are twelve truths about Father God2 (collated from Psalms 18, 23, 103, 121, 139, 145; Zephaniah 3; Matthew 6; Luke 15; John 13-17 and Romans 8).

Read them aloud slowly as a group:

My Father God, you are loving, good and trustworthy.

My Father God, you know everything about me and you run to welcome me.

My Father God, you have chosen me and adopted me into your family - you call me your son.

My Father God, you hold me close and call me by name.

My Father God, you rejoice over me and are proud of me as your child.

My Father God, you delight in me and enjoy being with me.

My Father God, you are patient and kind, you have forgiven me and you never give up on me.

My Father God, you are faithful. You know what I need before I ask you, and you provide everything I need.

My Father God, you guide and train me, giving me freedom to fail.

My Father God, you stand with me, you lift me up when I fall and turn my failures to good.

My Father God, you protect me and watch over my life.

My Father God, you are with me, you love me, and I belong to you.

Discuss:

Which of these truths about Father God had the greatest impact on you, and how?

Action:

In the group:

Take some time now in silent prayer, so that each person can talk to Father God about how and why this truth has affected them.

When you have finished talking directly with Father God, pray for each other in turn.

As you pray, ask the Holy Spirit to apply these truths about Father God to each person's mind, emotions and will.

Individually each day until the next Session:

- Read aloud the list of truths about Father God.

- Make a note of which truths impact you most.

- Talk to Father God about the impact of those truths, thanking him for his love and for making you his child.

A Prayer for each day:

Father God, thank you for lavishing your love on me.

Thank you for accepting me fully because of Jesus' sacrifice.

Thank you that I am secure because you love me,

Thank you that I am significant because I am your child,

You are amazing, Father God; and you are my Father.

Session 3: Brothers with a Purpose

Part 1: Social Time

 **Games:**

Drinks and Snack:

Part 2: Study Time

Explore:

Ask the group:

How did you get on reading the truths about Father God?

Which truths impacted you most?

What happened when you talked with Father God about these things?

How does it feel to know you are a child of God?

Focus 1

Read: Matthew 28:16-20

[16]Then the eleven disciples went to Galilee, to the mountain where Jesus had told them to go. [17]When they saw him, they worshipped him; but some doubted. [18]Then Jesus came to them and said, 'All authority in heaven and on earth has been given to me. [19]Therefore go and make disciples of all nations, baptising them in the name of the Father and of the Son and of the Holy Spirit, [20]and teaching them to obey

everything I have commanded you. And surely I am with you always, to the very end of the age.'

Think:

Jesus has completed his mission on earth.

He is about to return to His Father in heaven.

His disciples worship him as Lord. Some are hesitant, so Jesus reassures them about his supreme authority.

Then he gives them this incredible commission:

To continue making disciples, teaching these new disciples to do everything that Jesus has taught them.

We are in a long line of disciple-making which goes back almost 2000 years.

The commission Jesus gave then, rests on us today.

Our greatest purpose in life is to fulfil his commission.

Discuss:

What do you think and feel about being included in this great commission?

How helpful is it to know you are doing this together?

Focus 2

Read Micah 6:8

And what does the Lord require of you? 'To act justly and to love mercy and to walk humbly with your God'.

Think:

Loving other people equally is an important part of being a disciple of Jesus. Receiving this love from Christians often opens people's hearts to listen to what we say about Jesus.

Loving other people equally includes trying to achieve social justice, supporting the marginalised and standing up for those who are oppressed.

Discuss:

'Acting justly, loving mercy and walking humbly with God' - how important are these three attitudes in fulfilling Jesus' great commission?

How do your attitudes and actions each day demonstrate these Kingdom values?

How can we encourage each other to show this kind of love?

Action:

What small action can you take to show Jesus' love to someone?

Share this idea with the group, and pray for each other.

A Prayer for each day

Jesus, you humbled yourself and walked as a man on this earth,

Help me walk humbly with you today.

Jesus, you have shown me mercy and patience,

Help me be patient and show mercy to other people today.

Jesus, you were unafraid to right wrongs,

Help me be unafraid to do the same today. Amen.

Session 4: Copying Jesus

Part 1: Social Time

Games:

Drinks and Snack:

Part 2: Study Time

Explore:

Ask the group:

What do you think God thinks about you?

How does this affect your behaviour?

Focus:

Read: Luke 6:12-20

¹²One of those days Jesus went out to a mountainside to pray, and spent the night praying to God. ¹³When morning came, he called his disciples to him and chose twelve of them, whom he also designated apostles:

¹⁴Simon (whom he named Peter), his brother Andrew, James, John, Philip, Bartholomew, ¹⁵Matthew, Thomas, James son of Alphaeus, Simon who was called the Zealot, ¹⁶Judas son of James, and Judas Iscariot, who became a traitor.¹⁷

He went down with them and stood on a level place. A large crowd of his disciples was there and a great number of people from all over Judea, from Jerusalem, and from the coastal region around Tyre and Sidon, [18]who had come to hear him and to be healed of their diseases. Those troubled by impure spirits were cured, [19]and the people all tried to touch him, because power was coming from him and healing them all. [20]Looking at his disciples, he said: 'Blessed are you who are poor, for yours is the kingdom of God.

Think:

Jesus was in constant contact with his Father, of whom he spoke in very personal and intimate terms.

Prayer, praise and waiting on his Father were fundamental in the lifestyle of Jesus.

Jesus came as a human being and showed us the way human beings are to live their lives - in good relationship with God and with other people. We need each other.

After prayer, Jesus called the twelve to become his small group community and he spent up to three years building relationships with these disciples.

Notice how having prayed to his Father (UP) and gathered a team of people (IN) Jesus then moved out into the crowd doing the works of the Kingdom, sharing the Good News (OUT).

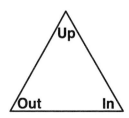

The triangle[3] is an easy way to remember this lifestyle of balance.

The pattern revealed in the life of Jesus shows us that to fulfill the great commission we first need to be in an intimate relationship with the Father (UP), also in relationship with one another (IN), as we move out to the world with the Good News (OUT).

Discuss:

Think about your life and the UP, IN, OUT, dimensions.

Which area are you strongest in, and which weakest?

Share this with your group. Do others in the group agree with you about that?

The lists on pages 32-33 give examples of things which can help develop the UP - IN - OUT areas.

Look at the list for the weakest area you have just identified - what could you do to strengthen that weak area?

How will you do it?

Share your thoughts with the group.

In the group agree on one or two actions (at the most) that each of you will commit to do in order to strengthen your weak area (UP, IN, or OUT).

Practices to help develop the 'UP'

A living relationship with Jesus grows as we spend time with him in daily commitment to spiritual disciplines like these:

Worship (alone and in a congregation).

Bible reading and study.

Prayer.

Meditation on the Scriptures.

Silence - listening to God.

Fasting.

Being open and aware of God's presence in the ordinary routines of life, especially at work.

Practices to help develop the 'IN'

Creating opportunities to meet with others in the church helps develop strong, open, caring relationships. These are some ideas that will develop this area:

Being hospitable.

Encouraging others with kind words and actions.

Working together on common projects/activities.

Playing games/ having fun time together.

Giving to others and receiving from others (e.g. time, money, skills, equipment, possessions).

Celebrating birthdays and other significant achievements.

Being honest about needs & worries, and asking friends for prayer/help.

Allowing others to speak honestly to us about our behaviour.

Practices to help develop the 'OUT'

We are the hands and feet of Jesus to the hungry, lonely, afflicted, homeless and abused. To grow more aware of the needs of those around you:

Walk prayerfully around your neighbourhood asking the Holy Spirit to open your eyes to the needs in the area.

Pray for your workplace. Expect God to give opportunities to build relationships or to share about your faith at work.

Become aware of not-yet Christians who are open and friendly to you in your neighbourhood and at work.

Make contact with the poor and marginalised - a smile or kind word is a start, perhaps join with others to give gifts to the poor - particularly at Christmas and Easter.

Notice strangers and see how you can bless/help them.

Look for and start to talk about issues of social justice in your community/workplace.

Stand up for women and girls who are being mistreated.

Make a stand against corruption and bribery.

 Action:

Put into action each day your plan to strengthen your weak area (UP-IN-OUT).

Pray daily for the other members of the group to be successful as they do this too.

Make contact with other group members to encourage each other.

A Prayer (try saying it slowly each day):

Father ... Abba ... Daddy ... Thank you
(repeat each word as often as you feel you need to)

May your blessing rest upon my brothers ...
(name before Father those who come to mind)

Lord Jesus Christ ... my Saviour ... my Friend ... my Brother
(repeat each word as often as you feel you need to)

May you be known as Saviour, Friend and Brother by ...
(name those who come to mind).
Amen.

Session 5: Called by Jesus to be a Band of Brothers

Part 1: Social Time

Games:

Drinks and Snack:

Part 2: Study Time

Explore:

Ask the group:

How did you get on with the action to strengthen your weakest corner of the triangle (UP - IN - OUT)?

How helpful was it being in contact to encourage and pray for each other?

Focus

Read: Luke 9:1-10

When Jesus had called the Twelve together, he gave them power and authority to drive out all demons and to cure diseases, ²and he sent them out to proclaim the kingdom of God and to heal those who were ill.

³He told them: 'Take nothing for the journey – no staff, no bag, no bread, no money, no extra shirt. ⁴Whatever house you enter, stay there until you leave that town. ⁵If people do not welcome you, leave their town and

shake the dust off your feet as a testimony against them.'

⁶So they set out and went from village to village, proclaiming the good news and healing people everywhere.

⁷Now Herod the tetrarch heard about all that was going on. And he was perplexed because some were saying that John had been raised from the dead, ⁸others that Elijah had appeared, and still others that one of the prophets of long ago had come back to life. ⁹But Herod said, 'I beheaded John. Who, then, is this I hear such things about?' And he tried to see him.

¹⁰When the apostles returned, they reported to Jesus what they had done. Then he took them with him and they withdrew by themselves to a town called Bethsaida.

Think:

Jesus has been training the 12 disciples by showing them how to preach the Good News of the Kingdom, how to heal the sick and how to deal with the demonic.

Notice how he sends them out in pairs.

When they return, he listens to their stories - their successes and their failures. He answers their questions and gives them feedback, before trying to take them away for a time of rest and reflection.

This is Jesus mentoring his followers together - as a team - so they not only learn from him, but learn through each other's experiences too.

Discuss:

Why does Jesus send the disciples out in pairs?

When they return, why does Jesus receive their feedback as a whole group and not in private with each individual?

What have you found helpful in listening to each other in the discussions so far?

Could this small group which you have been meeting in, be an important way in which Jesus is mentoring you together with other men, learning from him through each other?

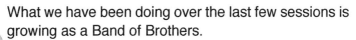

Think:

What we have been doing over the last few sessions is growing as a Band of Brothers.

A Band of Brothers following Jesus and growing together as friends.

This group - a Band of Brothers - is a safe place, where there is honest sharing and encouragement.

Together we are learning to hear Jesus and to be his disciples.

Action:

At the start of the meeting you talked about what you were doing to strengthen your weakest corner of the UP - IN - OUT triangle.

Share with your Band of Brothers what you will do to carry on strengthening your weakest area.

Ask them to lay hands on you and to pray for you now.

Agree to pray daily for each other, and to make contact with each other before the next meeting.

Reminder: Agree together the plan for the shared meal for the next Session.

Prayer:

Lord Jesus,

Thank you for all the things you have taught me since I became your follower.

I recognise that I am still learning from you.

Teach me to learn from you in partnership with my fellow disciples

Help me to walk with them and you in love and truthfulness.

I choose to open my heart to you and to your people.

Amen.

Session 6: Being a Band of Brothers

This final Session of Programme 1 has a different format.

Share a meal together.

Over the food ask one another these Band of Brothers Questions:

What do you remember most clearly from the Sessions?

What has changed in your life since you began meeting in this group?

What aspect of the balanced life, UP - IN - OUT, are you working on?

At the end of the meal pray for each other.

Agree the date you will start Programme 2, and how frequently you will meet.

Programme 2:

Discovering Jesus' Model of Evangelism

Welcome to Programme 2!

Special Instructions for Programme 2

Together as a Band of Brothers you will learn the model for evangelism that Jesus trained his followers to use, and start to use this for yourselves.

This model is for all followers of Jesus.

You will be learning together - just as the first disciples did - through each other's successes and disappointments.

Be prepared to both give and receive support from others in your Band of Brothers.

The Band of Brothers Questions

As a Band of Brothers you have been learning to trust each other. It is important to agree to keep confidential what others share.

Social Time

The 45 minutes social time before the Study Time is still vital to building friendship. You will learn more together if you do this.

Session 6, as in Programme 1, takes place around a meal. It needs to be prepared well ahead of time. This special session has its own format and focusses on explaining a Band of Brothers Strategy for Evangelism.

Session 1: Harvesters (not just seed sowers)

Part 1: Social Time

Games:

Drinks and Snack:

Part 2: Study Time

Band of Brothers Questions:

Ask the group:

What helped you most in Programme 1? How?

What are you looking forward to in Programme 2?

Focus:

Read: Luke 10:1-11

After this the Lord appointed seventy-two others and sent them two by two ahead of him to every town and place where he was about to go.

^{2}He told them, 'The harvest is plentiful, but the workers are few. Ask the Lord of the harvest, therefore, to send out workers into his harvest field.

^{3}Go! I am sending you out like lambs among wolves. ^{4}Do not take a purse or bag or sandals; and do not greet anyone on the road.

^{5}'When you enter a house, first say, "Peace to this house." ^{6}If someone who promotes peace is there, your peace will rest on them; if not, it will return to you. [7]Stay there, eating and drinking whatever they give you, for the worker deserves his wages. Do not move around from house to house.

[8]'When you enter a town and are welcomed, eat what is offered to you. [9]Heal those there who are ill and tell them, "The kingdom of God has come near to you." [10]But when you enter a town and are not welcomed, go into its streets and say, [11]"Even the dust of your town we wipe from our feet as a warning to you. Yet be sure of this: the kingdom of God has come near."

Think:

Jesus has a model for how to do evangelism and he teaches it to his disciples.

Earlier in Luke's gospel (chapter 9) Jesus has sent the twelve apostles out in pairs to spread the Good News of the Kingdom of God. Now he sends out 72 disciples in pairs, with the same instructions.

Notice that Jesus expects them to reap a plentiful harvest - not just to be sowing seeds!

The harvest is for God - it is his harvest field - and not for a particular person, organisation or church.

Discuss:

Imagine that you are one of the 72 hearing Jesus say the words in verses 3&4: *'I am sending you out like lambs among wolves. Do not take a purse or a bag or sandals ...'*

What do those words make you think and feel?

Why is it important to know that a plentiful harvest is possible?

Do you believe a plentiful harvest is possible among your family, friends, workplace or community?

Does this affect your attitude to sharing Jesus with them?

Do you need to make any changes to your attitudes, behaviour or lifestyle for that to happen?

 Action:

Your experience of evangelism in the past may have been disappointing. This may have affected how you feel about sharing your faith with others.

Read this prayer[4] of confession and forgiveness aloud together:

Father, how awesome and wonderful you are.

Lord, you are mighty and all powerful, the Creator of all.

Lord, your ways are higher than our ways,

Your thoughts higher than our thoughts.

Lord, I acknowledge you as the Lord of all.

Father, I give to you now my disappointment over past attempts at evangelism that did not go as well as I wanted … *(speak silently to the Lord).*

Lord, I confess I have held this against you and I am sorry.

I receive your forgiveness, Lord.

I recognise that now I do not see the picture of life clearly, but one day I shall see you face to face.

Now I know in part; then I shall know fully.

Lord, I recognise that I have focussed on what you didn't do instead of being thankful for all the things you did do.

I choose to trust in you and to follow you.

Please fill me with your Holy Spirit and with true faith in you.

In Jesus' name. Amen.

A Prayer for each day:

Pausing to talk to Jesus at different times in the day can help develop an awareness of Jesus' presence with us all the time.

Take this prayer into your workplace or home and use it whenever you have a drink - 'think it' to Father God, (you don't need to pray it out loud).

Jesus, as I hold this mug in my hands,

It reminds me that you hold my life in your hands.

You hold the lives of those around me in your hands too.

You know all our thoughts.

Jesus show me those whose hearts are open,

Those who are warming to your love and truth.

Open my eyes to see the harvest here.

And fill me with your boldness to do whatever you ask me to do for you. Amen.

Session 2: Being Vulnerable

Part 1: Social Time

Games:

Drinks and Snack:

Part 2: Study Time

Band of Brothers Questions:

Ask the group:

How did praying over your drink each day help you recognise Jesus' presence with you?

How helpful was it to break up your day with specific times of turning your attention to Jesus?

Focus:

Read: Luke 10:1-11

After this the Lord appointed seventy-two others and sent them two by two ahead of him to every town and place where he was about to go.

[2]He told them, 'The harvest is plentiful, but the workers are few. Ask the Lord of the harvest, therefore, to send out workers into his harvest field.

[3]Go! I am sending you out like lambs among wolves. [4]Do not take a purse or bag or sandals; and do not greet anyone on the road.

5"When you enter a house, first say, "Peace to this house." 6If someone who promotes peace is there, your peace will rest on them; if not, it will return to you. 7Stay there, eating and drinking whatever they give you, for the worker deserves his wages. Do not move around from house to house.

8"When you enter a town and are welcomed, eat what is offered to you. 9Heal those there who are ill and tell them, "The kingdom of God has come near to you." 10But when you enter a town and are not welcomed, go into its streets and say, 11"Even the dust of your town we wipe from our feet as a warning to you. Yet be sure of this: the kingdom of God has come near."

Think:

Jesus tells the 72 to go out on a mission trip without any supplies.

They will be totally dependent on other people - on strangers - to meet their needs for shelter and food.

They are vulnerable. They are dependent upon the hospitality of strangers.

But they trust Jesus who sent them and Father God to provide for their needs.

There was a cost to going in this way:

> If a village didn't like the message they brought, these men would spend a night or two sleeping in the open air and have no food until they received a welcome in another village.

This approach also created an opportunity:

> Being vulnerable is an invitation to another person to show their compassion - to open their hearts and help a person in need.

An open heart is a good place in which to sow the seed of the Gospel.

By inviting these travelling disciples to stay in their homes for a few days, their hosts didn't just get to *hear* the message they also got to *see* how disciples live, especially their attitudes and behaviour to each other and those around them.

Discuss:

Jesus asks his followers to take risks for him - to become vulnerable.

Can you remember doing something for Jesus that made you feel vulnerable?

By staying in peoples homes, the disciples in the story shared their whole lives.

Can you think of ways in which you can share the love and life of Jesus through your actions - without words?

How might that open up conversations about Jesus?

Taking risks for Jesus, becoming vulnerable, is not easy. Look at how some of the early disciples tackled this in their prayer in Acts 4:29-31:

²⁹Now, Lord, consider their threats and enable your servants to speak your word with great boldness. ³⁰Stretch out your hand to heal and perform signs and wonders through the name of your holy servant Jesus. ³¹After they prayed, the place where they were meeting was shaken. And they were all filled with the Holy Spirit and spoke the word of God boldly.

What do you think about praying like this - praying to be bold enough to be vulnerable?

 Action:

Pray for each other by laying hands on one another in turn and asking:

"Lord, please fill your servant with the Holy Spirit and enable your servant to speak your word with great boldness. Stretch out your hand to heal and perform miraculous signs and wonders through the name of your holy servant Jesus."

Agree to pray daily for each other, and to make contact to encourage each other before the next meeting.

A Prayer for each day

Lord Jesus, you promised, 'I am with you always',

and that means here, Lord!

'I am with you always', and that means today, Lord!

'I am with you always', and that includes me, Lord!

Thank you, Lord Jesus. Amen.

Session 3: Crossing Barriers

Part 1: Social Time

Games:

Drinks and Snack:

Part 2: Study Time

Band of Brothers Questions:

Ask the group:

How helpful was it to know your Band of Brothers were praying for you since the last meeting?

In what ways were you able to be bold and vulnerable?

Focus:

Read: Luke 10:1-9 and John 4:4-9

After this the Lord appointed seventy-two others and sent them two by two ahead of him to every town and place where he was about to go.

²He told them, 'The harvest is plentiful, but the workers are few. Ask the Lord of the harvest, therefore, to send out workers into his harvest field.

³Go! I am sending you out like lambs among wolves. ⁴Do not take a purse or bag or sandals; and do not greet anyone on the road.

⁵'When you enter a house, first say, "Peace to this

house." [6]If someone who promotes peace is there, your peace will rest on them; if not, it will return to you. [7]Stay there, eating and drinking whatever they give you, for the worker deserves his wages. Do not move around from house to house.

[8]'When you enter a town and are welcomed, eat what is offered to you. [9]Heal those there who are ill and tell them, "The kingdom of God has come near to you."'

Luke 10:1-9

[4]Now he had to go through Samaria. [5]So he came to a town in Samaria called Sychar, near the plot of ground Jacob had given to his son Joseph. [6]Jacob's well was there, and Jesus, tired as he was from the journey, sat down by the well. It was about noon.

[7]When a Samaritan woman came to draw water, Jesus said to her, 'Will you give me a drink?' [8](His disciples had gone into the town to buy food.)

[9]The Samaritan woman said to him, 'You are a Jew and I am a Samaritan woman. How can you ask me for a drink?' (For Jews do not associate with Samaritans.)

John 4:4-9

Think:

In the last Session we saw that Jesus expected his disciples to display vulnerability in order to share the Gospel. In this story Jesus himself demonstrates vulnerability in order to open up a conversation.

It is hot - nearly midday. Jesus has been walking for hours. He is tired and thirsty.

He stops at a well but he doesn't have a bucket. He needs help.

He breaks several cultural taboos to ask a Samaritan woman to give him a drink - things like:

Gender: Men and women who are strangers don't talk to each other.

Religion: They were from different religions. The Jews considered Samaritans ritually 'unclean' and thought that sharing eating and drinking vessels with Samaritans would make the Jewish person unclean too.

Race: They were from different ethnic/racial groups, and the Jews considered themselves superior to the Samaritans. It was demeaning for a Jew to ask a Samaritan for help.

Tradition: Jews and Samaritans were enemies and hostile to each other. For example, when Jews travelled through Samaria to Jerusalem for their religious festivals, Samaritans would often throw stones at them.

Jesus risks rejection by crossing these cultural barriers in order to bring the love of God to the woman.

At any point she could have ignored him, been rude or rejected his request.

 Discuss:

What barriers in your culture are there to talking or mixing with other people?

How might Jesus react to these barriers?

How do these barriers prevent you sharing the gospel more widely?

What social/religious/racial barriers are you prepared to cross in order to share the love of God with others?

How might others react to you crossing these barriers?

 Action:

Harvesting involves both listening to God's guidance about who is ready to hear the Gospel and being sensitive to where people are on their journey to faith.

Ask Jesus to bring to your mind right now the names or faces of people who need your prayers. Some of them may be 'across barriers' in your culture.

(Pause for silent prayer).

Now share these names with your group and then together pray for each person - that God would bless them and that they would come to know Jesus.

Before the next meeting continue to pray for these people and see what opportunities God opens up for you to connect with them - it may just be to say 'hello, how are you?'

A Prayer:

Jesus, thank you for crossing many barriers to save me.

Help me to go beyond my barriers and prejudices,

to share you with those who need to know you. Amen.

Session 4: Identifying our People of Peace

Part 1: Social Time

Games:

Drinks and Snack:

Part 2: Study Time

Band of Brothers Questions:

Ask the group:

In the last meeting you asked Jesus to bring to your mind the names or faces of people who needed your prayers. How have you got on praying for them?

Did God open up opportunities to serve them or talk with them?

Did you need to cross any cultural barriers?

How did you think and feel about that?

Focus:

Read: Luke 10:1-9

After this the Lord appointed seventy-two others and sent them two by two ahead of him to every town and place where he was about to go.

²He told them, 'The harvest is plentiful, but the workers

are few. Ask the Lord of the harvest, therefore, to send out workers into his harvest field.

[3]Go! I am sending you out like lambs among wolves. [4]Do not take a purse or bag or sandals; and do not greet anyone on the road.

[5]'When you enter a house, first say, "Peace to this house." [6]If someone who promotes peace is there, your peace will rest on them; if not, it will return to you.

[7]Stay there, eating and drinking whatever they give you, for the worker deserves his wages. Do not move around from house to house.

[8]'When you enter a town and are welcomed, eat what is offered to you. [9]Heal those there who are ill and tell them, "The kingdom of God has come near to you."

Think:

Notice Jesus tells his followers how to identify someone who may be open to the gospel:

> They welcome you.

> They act as a friend towards you and want to serve you.

> They act hospitably towards you - sharing their time and opening their home.

> These 'people of peace'[5] act as a gateway into their community for the disciples.

Jesus says that the Kingdom of God is close to these 'people of peace'.

He says that his rule and reign, his power and authority can come into their lives.

Jesus tells his followers to spend time with such people.

Discuss:

What are the characteristics of a 'person of peace'?

How could you identify people like this around you?

Can you identify someone who might right now be a 'person of peace' for you?

How will you respond to a 'person of peace'?

How could you open your life and give time to them so that they see the love and truth of Jesus in your life?

Action:

Share with the group the person who you think might be a person of peace for you.

Take time together to pray for these people.

Ask Jesus to confirm their warmth towards you before the next meeting; and think of a helpful way to respond that will bless them.

If no one has come to mind ask the group to pray for you to notice a person of peace in your life.

A Prayer for each day:

Father, may my friends and contacts know you, and what you are truly like.

Father, may my friends and contacts see that you really are good.

Father, provide for their daily needs.

Father, forgive me,

I freely forgive all who have annoyed me.

Father, let me see the 'people of peace' around me. Amen.

Session 5: Learning to Share your Story

Part 1: Social Time

Games:

Drinks and Snack:

Part 2: Study Time

Band of Brothers Questions:
Ask the group:

Did you notice any potential 'people of peace' since the last meeting?

How did you seek to bless and encourage them?

Why might this process take time to develop?

Can you think of any reasons/examples from your own journey to faith?

Focus:

Read: John 4:19-30, 39-42

[19]'Sir,' the woman said, 'I can see that you are a prophet. [20]Our ancestors worshipped on this mountain, but you Jews claim that the place where we must worship is in Jerusalem.'

[21]'Woman,' Jesus replied, 'believe me, a time is coming when you will worship the Father neither on this mountain nor in Jerusalem. [22]You Samaritans worship

what you do not know; we worship what we do know, for salvation is from the Jews. ²³Yet a time is coming and has now come when the true worshippers will worship the Father in the Spirit and in truth, for they are the kind of worshippers the Father seeks. ²⁴God is spirit, and his worshippers must worship in the Spirit and in truth.'

²⁵The woman said, 'I know that Messiah' (called Christ) 'is coming. When he comes, he will explain everything to us.' ²⁶Then Jesus declared, 'I, the one speaking to you – I am he.'

²⁷Just then his disciples returned and were surprised to find him talking with a woman. But no one asked, 'What do you want?' or 'Why are you talking with her?'

²⁸Then, leaving her water jar, the woman went back to the town and said to the people, ²⁹'Come, see a man who told me everything I've ever done. Could this be the Messiah?' ³⁰They came out of the town and made their way towards him....

³⁹Many of the Samaritans from that town believed in him because of the woman's testimony, 'He told me everything I've ever done.'

⁴⁰So when the Samaritans came to him, they urged him to stay with them, and he stayed two days. ⁴¹And because of his words many more became believers.⁴²They said to the woman, 'We no longer believe just because of what you said; now we have heard for ourselves, and we know that this man really is the Saviour of the world.'

Think:

We return to the story of Jesus' meeting with the woman at the well. Her encounter with Jesus was a turning point in her life.

She decides that Jesus is the Messiah and then quickly goes to the village to share her story of meeting him.

Her story enables others to encounter Jesus for themselves.

Discuss:

How did you come to know Jesus as Saviour and Lord?

What was life like before you met Jesus?

What is life like now that you are following him?

Action:

In answering the discussion questions you have just summarised your personal story of how you came to faith.

Pray for each other to have an opportunity to share your stories with someone who doesn't yet know Jesus.

Take some time to think about your story; what other things might it be helpful to include, or to leave out - depending on who you are telling it to?

Reminder: Agree together the plan for the shared meal for the next Session.

A Prayer for each day:

Thank you Lord for this new day of opportunity.

I say 'yes' to you Lord.

'Yes' to the opportunities to speak of you,

and 'yes' to living for you today. Amen.

Session 6: Band of Brothers Strategy for Evangelism

This final Session in Programme 2 has a different format.

Share a meal together

Have the discussion around the meal.

Over the meal ask these Band of Brothers Questions:

> Did you have opportunity to share your story with anyone - how did it go?

> Have you thought about your story - are there things you might change, and why?

Focus: Band of Brothers Strategy for Evangelism

Think:

We have been studying Jesus' evangelism strategy to reach the people in the villages and towns in the region of Galilee.

Below is a strategy for men to reach other men which uses many of the principles Jesus taught.

It has five levels, and each level draws men closer to Jesus at their own pace.

This strategy is common sense. As a Band of Brothers you have already been doing parts of it, and many churches implement some of it.

Band of Brothers Strategy

Level 1: Friendship in church

Create opportunities for the men in church to get together around fun activities. Friendships will develop and grow which will attract other men.

This is the foundation for everything else. Take time to develop real friendships. They are essential for effective outreach to men.

Level 2: Friendship beyond church

Invite contacts (family, work colleagues, neighbours) to the type of fun activities you have done in Level 1 - these must have zero 'Christian' content.

Yes - you did read that right - zero 'Christian' content.

For example try playing volleyball, cricket or frisbee ... or hire a minibus to go to watch a big game together.

This is a time to get to know each other. Be creative and keep it fun. Don't meet in church premises, as this may be difficult for some men.

Level 3: Share a faith story

When those taking part in Level 2 events have become relaxed as a group of friends, provide an opportunity for them to hear someone's faith story.

Host an event with a Christian speaker. Make the focus a meal. Choose someone with an interesting story about their work and life, and how Jesus is real to them.

This should not be preaching; it's sharing a personal story; something that will prompt men to think about Jesus.

Not everyone involved in Level 2 will be ready for Level 3 at the same time. Be patient and keep including them at Level 2 events.

Level 4: Run a 'finding out more' Course

For those men who want to find out more about Jesus and who have already been sharing life together at Level 1, 2 and 3 events.

There are some excellent courses available like 'Alpha' and 'Discovering Jesus through Asian eyes'. (For more information on these Courses see Appendix 3)

Men who aren't yet ready for this should not feel under any pressure to attend. Your friendship with them, and inclusion of them in Level 1, 2, and 3 events, should continue.

Level 5: Keep walking with Jesus together

Meet together regularly. Support, challenge and encourage each other - be a vibrant community excited by the message of Jesus.

Men like this make a positive difference to families, communities and workplaces.

 Discuss:

Which of the five levels is your Band of Brothers already doing?

Is this five level evangelism strategy useful for your Band of Brothers?

What will be your next step?

 Action:

At the end of the meal, pray for each other and decide a date to meet together to look at the 'Looking Forward' chapter.

A Prayer for each day:

Pray for each other, in the words that the apostle Paul used for Philemon:

"I pray that you may be active in sharing your faith,

so that you will have a full understanding

of every good thing that we have in Christ"

Paul's letter to Philemon v6

Looking Forward

Well done - you have completed this Toolkit!

You and your Band of Brothers have already been doing Levels 1, 3 and 5 of the Band of Brothers Evangelism Strategy and are now ready to try Levels 2 and 4.

It will be easy to add *Level 2 - Friendship beyond church.*

To do this as a group:

1. Choose the activity that would most appeal to your friends and contacts (your 'people of peace').

2. Decide on a date.

3. Encourage everyone to invite one or two contacts.

4. Enjoy!

After about 6 weeks arrange another Level 2 event.

In a few more weeks, when appropriate, introduce a *Level 3* activity for these 'people of peace'. *Level 3* activities usually take place two to three times a year.

Later some of the new group members may be ready for a *Level 4 'finding out more' Course.*

Use the Planning Sheet on page 70 to develop an annual or bi-annual programme of events to help lead the 'people of peace' Jesus has given you, to him.

Benjamin Francis is an experienced Indian evangelist and church planter. In 13 years he and his team have planted 10,500 churches. Benjamin gives these tips about evangelism[6]:

> First pray, make contact, deepen relationships ...
>
> then share your story and wait for God to show up ...

Planning Sheet for Five Level Evangelism

Month Actitivy	J a n	F e b	M a r	A p r	M a y	J u n e	J u l y	A u g	S e p t	O c t	N o v	D e c
Level 1: **Friendship in** **Church** (monthly - can be combined with level 5)												
Level 2: **Friendship** **beyond church** (4-5 times a year)												
Level 3: Share a **faith story** (2-3 times a year)												
Level 4: Run **a 'finding out** **more' Course** (once every 1-2 years)												
Level 5: Keep **walking with** **Jesus together** (weekly or fortnightly)												

Remember …

Evangelism to men requires long term commitment,
persistence and is based on authentic friendship.

For some resources that can be used to help develop the *Level 5*
'hands-on' discipleship, see Appendix 3.

Appendicees

Appendix 1: Notes

1. Polly House, *"Want your church to grow? Then bring in the men"*. Baptist Press News April 3rd 2003. www.bpnews. net/15630/want-your-church-to-grow-then-bring-in-the-men. Baptist Press, www.baptistpress.com.

2. This collation of truths about Father God was inspired by Neil Anderson's approach in *Steps to Freedom in Christ* (Oxford: Monarch Books 2000) 30. For more information: www.ficm.org. uk

3. Mike Breen and the 3DM team developed the concept of the Triangle - living a balanced life, as one of the 'Lifeshapes' discipleship tools. It is referenced in several 3DM publications including, Mike Breen, *Building a Discipling Culture* (Pawleys Island: 3DM 2011) 67-83. For more information: http:// www.3dmeurope.com/

4. Prayer dealing with 'Disappointment with God' © Marion Piper; modified with permission.

5. Mike Breen and the 3DM team developed the concept of the Person of Peace and relational mission, as one of the 'Lifeshapes' discipleship tools. It is referenced in several 3DM publications including, Mike Breen, *Building a Discipling Culture* (Pawleys Island: 3DM 2011) 153-163. For more information: http://www.3dmeurope.com/

6. Benjamin Francis, *"Tips for Evangelism"*: Engage, Autumn 2013www.bmsworldmission.org/engagecatalyst/engage-articles/top-ten-tips-evangelism. Engage is a BMS World Mission publication. www. bmsworldmission.org

Appendix 2: Leaders Notes

Leadership Style:

Your have the great privilege of walking with the men in your group as they make a journey of discovery about Jesus, and how he is discipling them ... and you.

Your role is to be a facilitator rather than a leader.

Jesus himself is the leader!

Being a facilitator is about helping the men to:

Recognise what Jesus is saying to them;

Work out what they are going to do about it;

Encourage each other to carry out their plan.

You have the additional privilege of leading by example, of modelling honesty and openness to the men in your group, especially about the things you are discovering as you walk with Jesus.

If you take the initiative to share your failures and disappointments, as well as the successes, then they will feel safe to share theirs too.

You are creating space for authentic friendships to develop.

Discussion Style:

The discussion time is really important. Your task is to help the group hear Jesus through the study materials and each other.

Then they can identify what their next step as a disciple of Jesus is, and the group can encourage and support each other in taking those steps.

The groups should have between 4 and 8 members, and as far as possible should be the same people for each Session. Remind the group that what is shared in the group must remain confidential.

In the studies there are no right or wrong answers! The answers will reflect where the men in the group are in their journey with Jesus.

Make space for everyone to share and ensure their contributions are valued. This is a group of equals and all deserve to be heard and respected.

If someone tries to dominate the group be polite but firm asking them to give others opportunity to speak. Remind everyone that you are a group of equals being discipled by Jesus. Keep in mind that even big issues are handled best by bringing them into the light, with love and truth.

Social Time Structure:

Games:

Choose something the men will enjoy doing together. Over the course of the two Programmes develop three or four favourite games that the group look forward to.

Variety will keep this section fresh and give different people the opportunity to excel at different games.

Drinks and Snacks:

Simple refreshments to keep everyone going, particularly if they have come to the group straight from work.

This is also an opportunity for chatting, getting to know each other better and catching up on news.

Study Time Structure:

Each of the Study Times has the following elements, with more than enought material for the 45 minutes.

Read Section:

The Bible passage should be read aloud from the book to help those who struggle with reading (and not from someone's preferred version). Make sure any person asked to read is happy to do so! It would be best to ask beforehand so they do not feel under any pressure.

Think Section:

This section draws out and clarifies points from the Bible passage. Read this slowly to the group. Allow them to ask questions to clarify their understanding. Then move on to ...

Discussion Section:

The sequence of the questions takes the group on a journey of discovery and discipleship.

There is more material than you will have time for. If you keep in your mind the question *"what is Jesus showing us here?"* it will help you select what to focus on.

Action Section:

This is where the ideas and decisions from the discussion section are turned into action plans. It is a vital part of each Session. So when you are preparing beforehand ensure you allocate sufficient time for it.

About the Explore Section:

In Session 3 of Programme 1, the 'Explore Section' is introduced at the start of the Study Time. In Programme 2 the 'Explore Section' is called 'Band of Brothers Questions' and features in all six Sessions.

These questions should be used to develop a sense of mutual care, support and trust among members of the Band of Brothers, as well as providing continuity between the Sessions. They are not a 'test'. The group are sharing in each others journey of discipleship.

About the Opportunities for Prayer:

Most Study Times include the opportunity to pray with or for each other.

Sensitivity is necessary because people are often hesitant about praying aloud in a group. Explaining that Christian prayer is talking with Father God in ordinary everyday language - a bit like chatting respectfully with your best friend - may help to put people at their ease.

Sometimes people can find it easier to write down their prayer before reading it aloud. So ensure that small sheets of paper and pens are available.

Over time the group will get to know each other better and recognise each others needs. This will generate compassion which will make praying for each other easier.

Leaders Study Time Notes for Programme 1:

Growing as a Band of Brothers

Programme 1 Session 1: Jesus is our Lord

Focus 1 Objective:

To recognise, like Peter, that we need to submit our lives entirely to Jesus as Saviour, finding forgiveness for our sins through him; and that when we do this, we discover new hope and a new purpose and direction in life.

Focus 2 Objective:

To recognise that we are called by Jesus into a journey following him; where we experience his friendship, and submit to his Lordship over us.

Action Objective:

For the men to start developing mutual understanding and concern for each other.

'What if' ... *you discover not all the men have given their lives to Jesus?*

Running this Toolkit may help them become disciples. Or if there are a significant number like this you may need to do a 'finding out more' Course first (see page 67) and then run this Toolkit later.

Programme 1 Session 2: God is our Father

Focus 1 Objective:

To prepare the men's emotions and minds for a deeper, more loving and trusting relationship with Father God - one that is far better than even the best human father-child relationship.

Focus 2 Objective:

To enter into a deeper relationship of love and trust with Father God by embracing the truth about him.

Action Objective:

Enable the men to immediately talk with Father God about what they have just discovered.

Encourage them to continue going deeper into the truth about Father God's character.

If all group members do not have a book, photocopies of the Truths about Father God should be made before you meet so that each person can take one away. To make this easier a single page version of these truths is overleaf (page 82)

'What if' ... *there is an emotional response (e.g. tears, joy or anger) to the Truths about Father God?*

First, relax, Father knows what he is doing.

Second, assure the man/men concerned that this release of emotion is OK. Encourage him/them to talk directly to Father God about how they are feeling and why they feel that way.

Be available to listen if they want to talk later.

Twelve Truths about Father God

Read them aloud slowly as a group:

My Father God, you are loving, good and trustworthy.

My Father God, you know everything about me and you run to welcome me.

My Father God, you have chosen me and adopted me into your family - you call me your son.

My Father God, you hold me close and call me by name.

My Father God, you rejoice over me and are proud of me as your child.

My Father God, you delight in me and enjoy being with me.

My Father God, you are patient and kind, you have forgiven me and you never give up on me.

My Father God, you are faithful. You know what I need before I ask you, and you provide everything I need.

My Father God, you guide and train me, giving me freedom to fail.

My Father God, you stand with me, you lift me up when I fall and turn my failures to good.

My Father God, you protect me and watch over my life.

My Father God, you are with me, you love me, and I belong to you.

(Collated from Psalms 18, 23, 103, 121, 139, 145; Zephaniah 3; Matthew 6; Luke 15; John 13-17 and Romans 8)

(This page is a photocopiable resource)

Programme 1 Session 3: Brothers with a Purpose

Explore Objective:

To grow in faith in God by listening to each others stories about how recognising Father God's character has impacted them.

Focus 1 Objective:

To recognise that Jesus' call is to fulfil his Great Commission, and that our lives have a much bigger purpose than just feeding ourselves, being successful and for some, bringing up a family.

Focus 2 Objective:

To understand that the spoken good news of the Kingdom of God goes hand in hand with the actions of social justice, standing up for the oppressed and being merciful. Also to recognise that real social and cultural changes flow from this Kingdom.

Action Objective:

To recognise that the decisions we take each day can bring the values and presence of the Kingdom of God into the lives of those around us - even if it is only in small ways, these are still significant.

'What if' ... *some men are overwhelmed by the challenge of the Great Commission?*

Encourage them that you are all in this together, and that the first disciples needed similar encouragement from Jesus - look at the reading from Matthew 28 again.

Programme 1 Session 4: Copying Jesus

Explore Objective:

To understand that God's love for us makes us significant and secure. Therefore we do not need to worry what other people think of us; we are free to show God's love to everyone.

'What if' ... *the response to the Explore questions is negative?*

As a group read aloud the truths about Father God from Session 2. Ask them to identify one truth which helps them recognise God's love for them.

Focus Objective:

To understand that we are meant to live a balanced life as Jesus did.

Action Objective:

For each person to have a plan of how to strengthen the weakest area of their life (UP, IN or OUT), and to encourage each other putting these plans into practice.

'What if' ... *some members of the group are reluctant to share openly and honestly about this.*

Firstly, don't take it personally. Jesus also encountered people who were not ready to hear what he had to say.

Secondly, for the protection of those who are sharing, remind the group that everything shared is to be kept confidential.

Thirdly, discipleship is an individual's choice; try to keep a positive and inclusive manner towards everybody.

Programme 1 Session 5: Called by Jesus to be a Band of Brothers

Explore Objective:

To recognise how helpful it is to have others encouraging us as we follow Jesus together.

Focus Objective:

To understand that Jesus' method of discipling his followers is as a group, so that we learn through each others experiences.

Action Objective:

For the group to be comfortable being accountable to each other and praying for each other.

NOTE: Agree the venue and arrangements for Session 6 which happens over a meal.

'What if' ... *there are personality clashes and friction within the group.*

Take heart - it happened among Jesus' group of 12 too!

We are part of God's family - in a family we don't get to choose who our brothers are.

Being disciples together includes recognising our difficulties and working through them honestly in relationship with Jesus and each other. Encourage the men to pray daily for those who they don't get on with - thanking God for something about them and asking God to bless them.

Programme 1 Session 6: Being a Band of Brothers

Objective:

For the group to appreciate how they have helped each other grow in faith, and to be motivated to continue the journey together in Programme 2.

'What if' ... *there is a signifiicant number who don't want to continue with Programme 2.*

Don't be defensive, but ask them to clarify why.

If you have sufficent men to continue with Programme 2 without them, press on.

You could suggest the others try out the first Session of Programme 2 before making their decision, but do make sure they understand that they cannot just join part way through the next Programme if they have missed the early Sessions.

If you don't have sufficient men to continue, talk with your church leaders and take their advice.

Leaders Study Time Notes for Programme 2:

Discovering Jesus' Model for Evangelism

Programme 2 Session 1: Harvesters (not just seed sowers)

Focus Objective:

For each of the men to believe in their hearts that people can come to faith in Jesus through them.

Action Objective:

To connect with Father God about past fears and disappointments, and to leave those fears behind.

What if ...*members of the group say they would not know what to say to evangelise others .*

This is a great place to be in!

Explain that it is the Holy Spirit who brings people to spiritual rebirth, not us. This Programme is designed to help us trust him and be involved in what the Holy Spirit is already doing in other men's lives.

In a later Session we will specifically look at how we can find the words to share our faith.

Programme 2 Session 2: Being Vulnerable

B of B Question Objective:

To recognise that Jesus is present with us everyday, in our ordinary lives, and that we can become more aware of his presence by turning our attention to him.

Focus Objective:

To recognise that being vulnerable is part of the walk of a disciple (remember, Jesus became a human being, born as a baby, in order to save us) and that our vulnerability can open people's hearts towards us and the Gospel.

Action Objective:

To be empowered by God-given boldness for witnessing about Jesus.

'**What if ...** *some in the group are frightened of the Holy Spirit working in and through them.*

Remind the group of the truths about Father God in Programme 1 Session 2. He is good and can be trusted.

The gift of the Holy Spirit in our lives - as Jesus present with us - is part of the new covenant promise, and is what defines us as children born of God. The Holy Spirit's enabling presence in us is the idea of a good Heavenly Father.

Programme 2 Session 3: Crossing Barriers

B of B Question Objective:

To understand that we can rely on each others support as we choose to be vulnerable in sharing the gospel.

Focus Objective:

To understand that not everything in our culture is right, and that as disciples of Jesus we should be prepared to cross the barriers that human beings put in place.

Note: Although the questions focus on crossing barriers, unhelpful breaches of gender barriers may put men and women at risk and damage the reputation of the church. Sexual sin is a possibility in any culture, and Session 3 is not encouraging men to engage in witnessing to women in private.

Action Objective:

For the men to actively listen to Jesus about those people around them who God is aready at work in by his Holy Spirit.

To develop the habit of cooperating with Jesus by praying for such people, and identifying opportunities to show love to them.

'**What if ...** *the group are unable to hear Jesus and are unable to pick up on any names or faces of people to pray for.*

Have the group sit quietly; thinking about: 'Father, your Kingdom come, your will be done ...'.

After some time encourage them to pray for the first person who comes to mind. Repeat this process a few times.

Programme 2 Session 4: Identifying our People of Peace

B of B Question Objective:

To recognise they are growing in understanding how to hear the Holy Spirit and to cooperate with him; this is both exciting and challenging, and we need wisdom and support from each other.

Focus Objective:

To develop the habit of regularly looking for the 'People of Peace' that Jesus is already working in.

Action Objective:

For the group to develop the habit of encouraging each other as they as they go about their normal lives as children of the living God.

'**What if ...** *the concept of identifying a 'person of peace' is too difficult for some in the group to grasp.*

Tell them not to worry. It will become clearer as the other group members feedback what has been happening to them.

This is part of the shared journey of discipleship - we learn different things at different speeds, and all benefit from listening to each other.

Programme 2 Session 5: Learning to Share your Story

B of B Question Objective:

To recognise that developing genuine friendship and mutual trust takes time.

It is important to be patient with ourselves and with those around us.

Focus Objective:

To help each person identify their own story of coming to know Jesus.

Action Objective:

To gain the confidence to share their own story of how they came to know Jesus and the difference he has made in their life.

To sympathetically listen to each others stories and encourage one another to recognise what Jesus is doing in and through them.

NOTE: Agree the venue and arrangements for Session 6 which happens over a meal.

'**What if ...** *some have grown up in Christian homes and struggle to identify a 'before' and 'after' knowing Jesus.*

Encourage them that what is important is knowing Jesus now. Ask them to think about the differences Jesus has made to their life and how they have changed over time because of being his followers. This is a story they can share.

Programme 2 Session 6: Band of Brothers Strategy for Evangelism

Objective:

For the group to understand the Band of Brothers Strategy for Evangelism, how the five levels work and how they can use the Strategy to provide a plan of activities and events that will help them lead other men to Jesus.

To agree a date to meet again to decide whether to commit time and energy to using this strategy to reach men.

If the group decide 'yes', the next step is to look at the 'Looking Forward' chapter together. This will help you develop a programme of activities around the Band of Brothers Strategy for Evangelism.

Appendix 3: Further Reading

Discipleship Tools:

Anderson, N.T. & Goss, S. *The Freedom in Christ Discipleship Course* (Oxford: Monarch, 2004).

Anderson, N. T. *Steps to Freedom in Christ* (Oxford: Monarch 2000)

Breen, M. *Building a Discipling Culture* (Pawleys Island: 3DM 2011)

Breen, M. *Multiplying Missional Leaders* (Pawleys Island: 3DM 2012)

Breen, M. *Leading Missional Communities* (Pawleys Island: 3DM 2013)

Breen, M. *Leading Kingdom Movements* (Pawleys Island: 3DM 2013) Information about 3DM at: *http://www.3dmeurope.com/*

Peterson, E. Johnson, J. Briggs J.R. Peckham, K. *The Message//Remix: Solo - An Uncommon Devotional* (Colorado Springs: NAVPress 2007)

'Finding out more' Courses

Alpha Course: www.alpha.org

Discovering Jesus through Asian Eyes: www.discovering-jesus.com

Academic Research about Jesus' Discipling Method:

Collinson, S. W. *Making Disciples: The Significance of Jesus' Educational Methods for Today's Church* (Milton Keynes: Paternoster, 2004).

The Discipling Models of the Post-Apostolic Church (and how they changed after Constantine made Christianity his religion):

Kreider, A. *'Baptism, Catechism and the Eclipse of Jesus' teaching in Early Christianity'* Tyndale Bulletin 47.2 (1996) 315-348.

Kreider, A. *The Change of Conversion and the Origin of Christendom.* (Christian Mission and Modern Culture), (Harrisberg: Trinity Press, 1999).

Ferguson, E. *'Catechesis and Initiation'* in Kreider, A. (ed.) The Origins of Christianity in the West. (Edinburgh: T&T Clark, 2001) 229-268.